The Powers of Angels

Prayers – Invocations

Translated by Judith Oringer

D.P. Marketing Editions
6, rue du Conseil Général
CH- 1205 Genève

2005, **D.P. Marketing** Editions

I.S.B.N.: 978-2-88492-027-8

David Phild

The Powers of Angels

Prayers – Invocations

Foreword

WHO ARE THE ANGELS?

Angels are intermediary beings, characteristic of the great monotheistic religions: Judaism, Christianity and Islam. The popularity of angels has grown over the last centuries, before almost totally disappearing after the Vatican II council. The current return of angels is an aspect of renewed spirituality.

A DIVINE MESSENGER

Angel comes from the Latin angelus, a translation of the Greek aggelos, which means: an envoy, a messenger, an emissary. It is used to translate the Hebrew mal'ak that has the ordinary meaning of messenger or ambassador and is used in the figurative sense to designate the angel of Yahweh or all beings that are part of his court.

Over the centuries, Christian and Jewish theologians conceived of a complex hierarchy of spiritual beings, and gave names to the most powerful of those that watched over humanity.

THE ANGELIC HIERARCHY

In its relationship with humanity, the angelic world is organized according to three perfect hierarchies. **Saint Denys** was the first, in the fourth century, to extract this revelation out of the Bible.

◆ The first hierarchy, the highest one, is made up of **Seraphim**, **Cherubim**, and **Thrones**.
They are so close to God that they receive his will over us directly from him, which they communicate to the inferior hierarchies. They are a bit like ministers for the king.

◆ The second hierarchy is made up of the **Dominations**, **Qualities** and **Powers.**
They generally see to it that divine will is applied to people. They are like the leadership of the king's army.

◆ The third hierarchy, that of the inferior angels, carries out God's commandments as far as we are concerned. They are like the king's army present on the field of combat. It is precisely because of their inferior nature that they can be so close to us.

This hierarchy is made up of angels of the order of the **Principalities**, in charge of the population's general destiny. They range from the order of the **Angel-Archangels** who announce great news and finally, to the **Angel-Angels or Guardian Angels** who take care of every individual in particular.

Chapter 1

GUARDIAN ANGELS:
instructions

How to find their name?

◆ Every guardian angel governs 5° of the zodiac and the 5 days of the year that correspond to these degrees.

◆ Therefore, the people born on these 5 days have this angel as their guardian angel.

◆ It's even simpler yet: every sign of the zodiac is governed by 6 guardian angels.

◆ All you have to do then is to look for the chapter that corresponds to your sign and you will quickly find your guardian angel: the one that corresponds to your date of birth.

Male or female?

Contrary to popular opinion, the sex of angels is well-defined in the Cabala (the esoteric side of the Bible).

In fact, everything in the Universe has a positive or negative pole, male or female: the angels are no exception.

◆ Guardian angels that have the name of God in its masculine sense: **EL** have masculine characteristics.
◆ Guardian angels that have the name of god in its feminine sense: **IAH** have feminine characteristics.

When to call upon him?

◆ Every day, without exception but for very important requests, the day of your birthday is favored.

How to call upon him?

◆ By his name and his prayer. Those I recommend to you are not words from the gospel, you can adapt them to your specific request and with your words, those that come from the heart. However, you should know that...
❒ Guardian angels don't like familiarity.
❒ They appreciate pretty metaphors.
❒ A few candles, incense and beautiful music — classical or mind-blowing — attracts them irresistibly.
❒ They are also very sensitive to being thanked after any request for an intervention.

Can one call upon someone else's guardian angel?

◆ No problem. Every guardian angel actually has special powers and can also be called upon.

How?

◆ Either by asking your guardian angel to intercede for you with his colleague.
◆ Or by contacting him directly, on the days and hours on duty that you will find on every angel sheet.

Chapter 2

THE SIX ANGELS OF ARIES

If you were born between
March 21 and April 21,
your guardian angel is
one of the 6 angels of Aries
and belongs to
the Choir of the Seraphim.
Quickly find out his nickname,
his special powers,
and how to pray to him
to obtain his favors.

You were born between March 21 and 25
Your Guardian angel is

1- Véhuiah

HIS ARCHANGEL
Metatron

HIS IDENTITY

Gender Female

Family Seraphim

HIS AFFINITIES

Stone Amethyst

Candle Violet

Incense Lilac

Powder Iris

VÉHUIAH symbolised **transformation**. He gives you strength and willpower as well as love, clarity and wisdom.

Véhuiah awakens your intuition and brings you success for all new projects, in love or business.

Even if he is not your guardian angel, you can call upon him for:

◆ Passing a test
◆ A job interview
◆ Enhancing the beginning of a love relationship.

Prayer to Véhuiah

*Véhuiah, instill in me
the spirit of decision-making and will power
that are part of your divine essence.*

*Enable me to express the gifts
that will ensure success
in everything I undertake.*

*Grant me the energy that will allow me
to advance in my spiritual
and material quest.*

You were born between March 26 and 30
Your Guardian Angel is

2- *Jeliel*

HIS ARCHANGEL
Métatron

HIS IDENTITY

Gender Male

Family Seraphim

HIS AFFINITIES

Stone Fluorite

Candle Mauve

Incense Armoise

Powder Gardenia

J ELIEL symbolizes **fecundity** and **fertility** for three kingdoms: animal, vegetable and human. He watches over the couple's faithfulness and solidity. Jéliel breathes into his protégés invigorating energy and a sense of responsibility. You can call upon him, even if he is not your guardian angel for:

◆ Making a project concrete.
◆ Building your house.
◆ Creating a family.
◆ Winning at a trial.

When to call upon Jeliel?

◆ If Jeliel is your Guardian Angel, you can call upon him and pray to him every day for him to dispense his good deeds on you.

◆ If Jeliel is not your Guardian angel, you can call upon him on his days of regency and 20 minutes every day (see below).

March 22
June 4
August 18
October 30

January 10
Every day
from 12:20 AM
to 12: 40 AM

Prayer to Jeliel

Jeliel, help me dominate
my instincts and follow the voice
of my conscience, in all circumstances.

Offer me your divine protection
for success and well-being
in my couple relationship and my family.

Make a fertile field of my life
where the good grain supplants the rye grass and
where love flourishes without ever withering.

You were born between March 31 and April 4. Your Guardian Angel is

3- Sitael

HIS ARCHANGEL
Métatron

HIS IDENTITY

Gender Male

Family Seraphim

HIS AFFINITIES

Stone Opal

Candle Pearly

Incense Cinnamon

Powder Eucalyptus

S ITAEL symbolizes **responsibility**. He opens up access to important posts in decision-making and power to his protégés.

Sitael protects you from anxiety, armed attacks and evil powers. He also teaches you how to have your wealth be productive. Even if he is not your guardian angel you can call upon him for:

◆ Finding a soul mate.
◆ Getting a promotion.
◆ Overcoming adversity.

When to call upon Sitael?

◆ If Sitael is your Guardian Angel, you can call upon him and pray to him every day for him to dispense his good deeds on you.

◆ If Sitael is not your Guardian angel, you can call upon him on his days of regency and 20 minutes every day (see below).

March 23
June 5
August 19
October 31

January 11

Every day from 12:40 AM to 1 AM

Prayer to Sitael

Sitael, bring me peace in my heart and spirit so that each of my decisions is the right one and not dictated by emotions or resentment.

Protect me as well as all those who are dear to me from physical, moral or occult attacks so that I may be fulfilled in love and dignity.

You were born between April 5 and 9
Your Guardian Angel is

4- Élémiah

HIS ARCHANGEL
Métatron

HIS IDENTITY
Gender Female

Family Seraphim

HIS AFFINITIES
Stone Jade

Candle Pale green

Incense Lotus

Powder Honeysuckle

ELEMIAH symbolizes **success** and **protection**. He stimulates his protégés to show themselves to be valiant and ardent in accomplishing their tasks. An ecological angel, Élémiah guides those who have the desire to preserve the natural richness and energies of our planet in their heart.

Even if he is not your guardian angel, you will call upon him for:

◆ Avoiding all excess.
◆ Obtaining wealth and power.
◆ Protecting yourself from accidents.

When to call upon Élémiah?

◆ If Élémiah is your Guardian Angel, you can call upon him and pray to him every day for him to dispense his good deeds on you.

◆ If Élémiah is not your Guardian angel, you can call upon him on his days of regency and 20 minutes every day (see below).

March 24   **January 12**
June 6
August 20   **Every day from**
November 1   **1 AM to 1:20 AM**

Prayer to Élémiah

Élémiah, guide me on the paths
of success without my being prey
to an ambition that would be degrading.

Protect me from excess, negligence
and lack of attention so that
I may avoid all accidents.

Help me in my struggle to
protect nature and
endangered species.

You were born between April 10 and 14
Your Guardian Angel is

5- *Mahasiah*

HIS ARCHANGEL
Métatron

HIS IDENTITY

Gender Male

Family Seraphim

HIS AFFINITIES

Stone   Sapphire

Candle   Cobalt blue

Incense Citron

Powder   Verbena

MAHASIAH symbolizes **peace and harmony**. He awakens the ego in a dimension of plenitude. Mahasiah gives his protégés access to high-level knowledge by means of initiation. He also inspires those who exercise professional or artistic professions. Even if he is not your guardian angel, you will call upon him for:

◆ Getting your health back.
◆ Acquiring knowledge.
◆ Enhancing your creativity.
◆ Becoming an awakened being.

When to call upon Mahasiah?

◆ If Mahasiah is your Guardian Angel, you can call upon him and pray to him every day for him to dispense his good deeds on you.

◆ If Mahasiah is not your Guardian angel, you can call upon him on his days of regency and 20 minutes every day (see below).

March 25
June 7
August 21
November 2

January 13

**Every day from
1:20 AM to 1:40 AM**

Prayer to Mahasiah

*Mahasiah, appease my heart and soul
so that I may reconcile myself with
the people who are dear to me from whom
I am estranged.*

*Open up for me the world of ideas
so that I may develop
all the facets of my creativity
harmoniously.*

*Help me find the path
of knowledge and spiritual awakening.*

You were born between April 15 and 20
Your Guardian Angel is

6- Léhahel

HIS ARCHANGEL
Métatron

HIS IDENTITY

Gender Male

Family Seraphim

HIS AFFINITIES

Stone Turquoise

Candle Blue/green

Incense Lemon grass

Powder Tuberose

L ÉHAHEL symbolizes **health** and a **fast cure** from illnesses. He grants his protégés faith and fortune in the world of the sciences and the arts. He enhances beauty, physical radiance and the development of magnetism.

Even if he is not your guardian angel, you will call upon him for:

◆ Attaining glory.
◆ Making a wealthy marriage.
◆ Curing one's fellow creatures.

When to call upon Léhahel?

◆ If Léhahel is your Guardian Angel, you can call upon him and pray to him every day for him to dispense his good deeds on you.
◆ If Léhahel is not your Guardian angel, you can call upon him on his days of regency and 20 minutes every day (see below).

March 26	**January 14**
June 8	
August 22	**Every day from**
November 3	**1:40 AM to 2 AM**

Prayer to Léhahel

*Léhahel, give me the strength
and generosity I need to relieve,
in abnegation and love,
those who suffer, whether they are
friends or simple passersby.*

*Help me to banish selfishness, vanity
and a taste for money from my life
and to share the privileges that Heaven
has granted me in a spirit
of justice and solidarity.*

Chapter 3

THE 6 ANGELS OF TAURUS

If you were born between
April 22 and May 21,
your guardian angel is
one of the 6 angels of Taurus
and belongs either
to the Choir of the Seraphim,
or the Choir of the Cherubim.
Quickly find out his nickname,
his special powers,
and how to pray to him
to obtain his favors.

You were born between April 21 and 25
Your Guardian Angel is

7- Achaiah

HIS ARCHANGEL
Métatron

HIS IDENTITY

Gender Female

Family Seraphim

HIS AFFINITIES

Stone Pearl

Candle Parma

Incense Nutmeg

Powder Violet

ACHAIAH symbolizes **understanding** and **faith**. This angel with a feminine nature gives his protégés discernment and patience. He puts them in osmosis with the forces of nature and enhances creativity in all its forms.

Even if he is not your guardian angel, you can call upon him for:

◆ Stimulating your intelligence.
◆ Discovering a secret truth.
◆ Enhancing communication.

When to call upon Achaiah?

◆ If Achaiah is your Guardian Angel, you can call upon him and pray to him every day for him to dispense his good deeds on you.

◆ If Achaiah is not your Guardian angel, you can call upon him on his days of regency and 20 minutes every day (see below).

March 27   January 15
June 9
August 23 and 24   Every day from
November 4   2 AM to 2:20 AM

Prayer to Achaiah

Achaiah, fill me with your light
to show me the road of truth.
Protect me from the poison of jealousy
and temptations from the Darkness.

Open up my field of awareness
so that I may communicate
in respect and harmony,
with all beings living on this earth.

You were born between April 26 and 30
Your Guardian Angel is

8- Cahetel

HIS ARCHANGEL
Métatron

HIS IDENTITY

Gender Male

Family Seraphim

HIS AFFINITIES

Stone Fluorite

Candle Rose

Incense Thyme

Powder Armoise

CAHETEL symbolizes the **harvest** and **prosperity**. He is the angel of water and the home. He stimulates his protégés to experience the simple things in life and inculcates in them the values of justice and respect. You can call upon him, even if he is not your guardian angel for:

◆ Finding your love nest.
◆ Discovering a spring of water.
◆ Fertilizing a sterile belly.
◆ Giving yourself prosperity.

When to call upon Cahetel?

◆ If Cahetel is your Guardian Angel, you can call upon him and pray to him every day for him to dispense his good deeds on you.

◆ If Cahetel is not your Guardian angel, you can call upon him on his days of regency and 20 minutes every day (see below).

March 28   **January 16**
June 10
August 25   **Every day from**
November 5   **2:20 AM to 2:40 AM**

Prayer to Cahetel

*Cahetel, I appeal to you so that
my home is and remains, as time goes along,
the special place where I can recharge
my energy in peacefulness and well-being.*

*Help me to keep my eyes full of wonder
like a child's all my life long.
Enable me to find happiness
in the simple things of life
and protect me from the odorless song
of the sirens.*

You were born between May 1 and 5
Your Guardian Angel is

9- *Haziel*

HIS ARCHANGEL
Raziel

HIS IDENTITY

Gender Male

Family Seraphim

HIS AFFINITIES

Stone Amazonite

Candle Orange

Incense Cedar

Powder Carnation

HAZIEL symbolizes **forgiveness** and **unconditional love**. He develops a curious, inventive spirit in his protégés. He invites them to put the strength of their spirit in the service of humanitarian aid.

You can call upon Haziel, even if he is not your guardian angel for:

◆ Recovering affection.
◆ Forgiving and being forgiven.
◆ Finding your other half.
◆ Finding peace in your heart.

When to call upon Haziel?

◆ If Haziel is your Guardian Angel, you can call upon him and pray to him every day for him to dispense his good deeds on you.

◆ If Haziel is not your Guardian angel, you can call upon him on his days of regency and 20 minutes every day (see below).

March 29	**January 17**
June 11	
August 26	**Every day from**
November 6	**2:40 AM to 3:00 AM**

Prayer to Haziel

Haziel, merciful angel,
help me pacify my heart,
forgive those who have offended me
and be forgiven by those I have made suffer.

Make a garden of roses of my life with
a thousand fragrances so that in turn,
I may offer beauty, love and compassion
to those who only know suffering
and destitution.

You were born between May 6 and 10
Your Guardian Angel is

10- Aladiah

HIS ARCHANGEL
Raziel

HIS IDENTITY

Gender Female

Family Cherubim

HIS AFFINITIES

Stone Aventurine

Candle Silver

Incense Cypress

Powder Hyacinth

ALADIAH symbolizes **forgiveness for bad actions and a cure for illnesses.** He guides those who have been on the wrong path and who have the strength to recognize their errors and adapt another way of living.

You can call upon Aladiah even if he is not your guardian angel for :

◆ Getting out of an impasse.
◆ Freeing yourself from the past.
◆ Being cured.
◆ Enhancing your magnetism.

When to call upon Aladiah?

◆ If Aladiah is your Guardian Angel, you can call upon him and pray to him every day for him to dispense his good deeds on you.

◆ If Aladiah is not your Guardian angel, you can call upon him on his days of regency and 20 minutes every day (see below).

March 30   January 18
June 12
August 27   Every day from
November 7   3 AM to 3:20 AM

Prayer to Aladiah

Aladiah, help me stop wandering off onto unproductive paths which have made a pariah out of me in the past.

Grant me forgiveness for my previous errors and wipe out this karmic debt which makes me vulnerable to illness and exclusion.

I desire, with all my soul, to go back on the road of light, health and honor.

You were born between May 11 and 15
Your Guardian Angel is

11- Lauviah

HIS ARCHANGEL
Raziel

HIS IDENTITY

Gender Male

Family Cherubim

HIS AFFINITIES

Stone Hematite

Candle Red

Incense Amber

Powder Red rose

L AUVIAH symbolizes **wisdom and fame**. He grants his protection against disasters, whether they are natural or personal. Lauviah bids his protégés to awaken themselves with confidence and optimism to the qualities of the spirit.

You can call upon him even if he is not your guardian angel for:

◆ Having a talent be recognized.
◆ Succeeding socially.
◆ Finding meaning for your life.

When to call upon Lauviah?

◆ If Lauviah is your Guardian Angel, you can call upon him and pray to him every day for him to dispense his good deeds on you.

◆ If Lauviah is not your Guardian angel, you can call upon him on his days of regency and 20 minutes every day (see below).

March 31	**January 19**
June 13	
August 28	**Every day from**
November 8	**3:20 AM to 3:40 AM**

Prayer to Lauviah

Lauviah, enable me to develop
these talents, fruits of divine providence
so that they don't remain fallow
and can blossom in broad daylight.

Help me, beautiful angel of wisdom,
to attain the highest peaks
not in a spirit of pride or riches
but of praise, gratitude and sharing.

You were born between May 16 and 20
Your Guardian Angel is

12- Hahaiah

HIS ARCHANGEL
Raziel

HIS IDENTITY

Gender Male

Family Cherubim

HIS AFFINITIES

Stone Pyrite

Candle Orange

Incense Pine

Powder Peony

 AHAIAH symbolizes **revelation and occult protection**. The refuge angel (his nickname) gives his protégés the ability to interpret their dreams and supernatural signs. Occultism and psychology will therefore be your favorite domains.

You will call upon Hahaiah even if he is not your guardian angel for:

◆ Developing your intuition.
◆ Having a dialogue with the beyond.
◆ Protecting yourself from attacks.

Prayer to Hahaiah

*Hahaiah, help me to develop
my intuitive ability and to use it fully,
so I can enlighten
my fellow man with honesty and rigor.*

*Grant me your protection and light
so I can avoid the pitfalls and attacks
that line the road of those
who seek contact with other planes.*

Chapter 4

THE 6 ANGELS OF GEMINI

If you were born between
May 22 and June 21,
your guardian angel is
one of the 6 angels of Gemini
and either belongs to
the Choir of the Cherubim,
or the Choir of the Thrones.
Quickly find out his nickname,
special powers,
and how to pray to him
to obtain his favors.

You were born between May 21 and 25
Your Guardian Angel is

13- Iezalel

HIS ARCHANGEL
Raziel

HIS IDENTITY
Gender Female
Family Cherubim

HIS AFFINITIES
Stone Granite
Candle Incarnate
Incense Juniper
Powder Rue

I EZALEL symbolizes **reconciliation and fidelity**. He gives his protégés a sense of respect for their commitments and of responsibility. He encourages them to ask themselves the right questions and to cultivate authenticity with determination.

Even if Iezalel is not your guardian angel, you can call upon him for:

◆ Creating a unified couple.
◆ Resolving conflicts.
◆ Overcoming intolerance.

Prayer to Iezalel

Iezalel, give me the wisdom and clarity
I need to distinguish authentic values
and to learn to respect them.

Sharpen my mind with justice and peace
so that I may become the mediator of spirits
that wander and useless conflicts.

Give me fidelity in body and heart
so that I may live serenely in honor,
respect and love.

You were born between May 26 and 31
Your Guardian Angel is

14- Mébahel

HIS ARCHANGEL
Raziel

HIS IDENTITY

Gender Male

Family Cherubim

HIS AFFINITIES

Stone Agate

Candle Light brown

Incense Amber

Powder Heather

MÉBAHEL symbolizes **rectitude and justice**. A justice that is meant to be benevolent, tolerant and that help to free oppressed and innocent prisoners. He grants his protégés fame in exercising rights.

You can call upon Mébahel even is he is not your guardian angel for:

◆ Defending a cause.
◆ Winning at a trial.
◆ Passing a test.

When to call upon Mébahel?

◆ If Mébahel is your Guardian Angel, you can call upon him and pray to him every day for him to dispense his good deeds on you.

◆ If Mébahel is not your Guardian angel, you can call upon him on his days of regency and 20 minutes every day (see below).

April 3	**January 22**
June 17	
August 31	**Every day from**
November 11	**4:20AM to 4:40 AM**

Prayer to Mébahel

Mébahel, angel of justice and peace,
give me the ability to recognize
and defend just causes
since that is my vocation.

Don't let my emotions, my pride
or my interests denature the truth.

Grant me benevolence and compassion
for making legitimate rights triumph
even for the very humblest people.

You were born between June 1 and 5
Your Guardian Angel is

15- Hariel

HIS ARCHANGEL
Raziel

HIS IDENTITY

Gender Male

Family Cherubim

HIS AFFINITIES

Stone Malachite

Candle Orange

Incense Mistletoe

Powder Bay leaf

HARIEL symbolizes **faith that has been restored** after a period of doubt and **freedom from bad habits** that were acquired in torment. Hariel guides those who have a taste for discovery, such as explorers or scientists.

You can call upon Hariel even if he is not your guardian angel for:

◆ Affirming your faith.
◆ Finding your way.
◆ Succeeding in withdrawal.

When to call upon Hariel?

◆ If Hariel is your Guardian Angel, you can call upon him and pray to him every day for him to dispense his good deeds on you.

◆ If Hariel is not your Guardian angel, you can call upon him on his days of regency and 20 minutes every day (see below).

April 4	**January 23**
June 18	
September 1	**Every day from**
November 12	**4:40 AM to 5:00 AM**

Prayer to Hariel

*Hariel, help me recover my faith
in myself, in others and in
my convictions or beliefs.*

*Enable me to overcome all forms
of dependencies that darken my soul
and have turned me away from the light.*

*Guide me towards new discoveries
made of joys, exchanges and friendship
to give positive meaning to my life.*

You were born between June 6 and 10
Your Guardian Angel is

16- Hekamiah

HIS ARCHANGEL
Raziel

HIS IDENTITY

Gender Female

Family Cherubim

HIS AFFINITIES

Stone Lapis Lazuli

Candle Orange

Incense Musk

Powder Mimosa

H EKAMIAH symbolizes **the grace and friendship** you can find in well-known figures who are on a high level, and who have power and fame. He will bring you fame, while developing your ability with relationships and your gifts of persuasion.

You can call upon Hekamiah even if he is not your guardian angel for:

◆ Being in politics.
◆ Becoming a decision-maker.
◆ Creating relationships.

When to call upon Hekamiah?

◆ If Hekamiah is your Guardian Angel, you can call upon him and pray to him every day for him to dispense his good deeds on you.

◆ If Hekamiah is not your Guardian angel, you can call upon him on his days of regency and 20 minutes every day (see below).

April 5	**January 24**
June 19	
September 2	**Every day from**
November 13	**5:00 AM to 5:20 AM**

Prayer to Hekamiah

Hekamiah, give me the charisma
I need to get my ideas across
to people who are indispensable
in making my projects succeed.

Enable me to steer a delicate course
in the corridors of power and to attain
my goals while remaining full of integrity,
with neither complacency nor compromises.

17- Lauviah (2)

HIS ARCHANGEL
Binael

HIS IDENTITY

Gende Female

Family Thrones

HIS AFFINITIES

Stone Carnelian

Candle Indigo

Incense Jasmine

Powder Angelica

L AUVIAH symbolizes **abnegation, the gift of self**. He stimulates his protégés to relieve those who are in suffering and inspires them with the sense of sacrifice. Lauviah (2) also inspires those who write in the area of psychology.

You can call upon Lauviah (2) even if he is not your guardian angel for:

◆ Enhancing a vocation.
◆ Learning how to receive.
◆ Letting yourself be loved.

When to call upon Lauviah (2)?

◆ If Lauviah (2) is your Guardian Angel, you can call upon him and pray to him every day for him to dispense his good deeds on you.

◆ If Lauviah (2) is not your Guardian angel, you can call upon him on his days of regency and 20 minutes every day (see below).

April 6	**January 25**
June 20	
September 3	**Every day from**
November 14	**5:20 AM to 5:40 AM**

Prayer to Lauviah (2)

Lauviah, you who have inspired me
with compassion, love as an offering
and with self-effacement,
also teach me how to receive carnal love,
in an uncomplicated way.

Even if listening to others is often
enough for my happiness,
loneliness weighs down on me
and my dearest desire is to reenergize myself
in the sweetness of a home.

47

You were born between June 16 and 21
Your Guardian Angel is

18- Caliel

HIS ARCHANGEL
Binael

HIS IDENTITY

Gender Male

Family Thrones

HIS AFFINITIES

Stone Studded ruby

Candle Coral

Incense Reseda

Powder Mistletoe

CALIEL symbolizes **truth and justice**. He inspires in his protégés rigor and an acute sense of equity, which will work wonders at the bar, in charitable or humanitarian work. Caliel brings quick aid in adversity. You can call upon Caliel even if he is not your guardian angel for:

◆ Proving your innocence.
◆ Recovering what is owed to you.
◆ Finding help and assistance.
◆ Asserting your rights.

When to call upon Caliel?

◆ If Caliel is your Guardian Angel, you can call upon him and pray to him every day for him to dispense his good deeds on you.

◆ If Caliel is not your Guardian angel, you can call upon him on his days of regency and 20 minutes every day (see below).

April 7
June 21
September 4
November 15

January 26

Every day from
5:40 AM to 6:00 AM

Prayer to Caliel

Caliel, angel of truth, open up my eyes,
under all circumstances, so that the causes
that I might be brought to defend
are just ones and in the order of the Law.

And if I have taken a wrong path
and live in disapproval or destitution
bring me your help and your light
so that I can quickly get out of this impasse.

Chapter 5

THE 6 ANGELS OF CANCER

If you were born between
June 22 and July 22,
your guardian angel is
one of the 6 angels of Cancer
and belongs to the Choir of Thrones.
Quickly discover his nickname,
his special powers,
and how to pray to him
to obtain his favors.

19- Leuviah

HIS ARCHANGEL
Binael

HIS IDENTITY

Gender Female

Family Thrones

HIS AFFINITIES

Stone Chrisoprase

Candle Blue

Incense Dragon's blood

Powder Garlic

L EUVIAH symbolizes **letting go strategically**, which brings victory over adversity. It fulfills he who surrenders to providence for settling his accounts with blessings. He also has a calling for refreshing your memory.

Even if Leuviah is not your guardian angel, you can call upon him for:

◆ Confounding evil people.
◆ Refining your strategies.
◆ Reviving your memories.

When to call upon Leuviah?

◆ If Leuviah is your Guardian Angel, you can call upon him and pray to him every day for him to dispense his good deeds on you.

◆ If Leuviah is not your Guardian angel, you can call upon him on his days of regency and 20 minutes every day (see below).

April 8	**January 27**
June 22	
September 5	**Every day from**
November 16	**6:00 AM to 6:20 AM**

Prayer to Leuviah

*Leuviah, I surrender to you to calm
my impulses for vengeance and for punishing
in my name those who have offended me.*

*Awaken my memory to facilitate
my professional life but erase from your
angel's feather all desire for revenge.*

*I know that this renouncement is not in vain
for banishing negative emotions is the
only path for entering into the light.*

You were born between June 27 and July 1
Your Guardian Angel is

20- Pahaliah

HIS ARCHANGEL
Binael

HIS IDENTITY
Gender Female

Family Thrones

HIS AFFINITIES
Stone Tourmaline

Candle Cobalt blue

Incense Amber

Powder Camellia

P AHALIAH symbolizes **vocation**. He controls religious, humanitarian or charitable vocations. Ordeals are experienced simply as challenges where the point is to learn the lesson from it. A fruitful, energizing experience that transcends fears and anxieties.

You will call on Pahaliah, even if he is not your guardian angel for:

◆ Overcoming your anxieties.
◆ Affirming a vocation.
◆ Winning at a challenge.

When to call upon Pahaliah?

◆ If Pahaliah is your Guardian Angel, you can call upon him and pray to him every day for him to dispense his good deeds on you.

◆ If Pahaliah is not your Guardian angel, you can call upon him on his days of regency and 20 minutes every day (see below).

April 9
June 23
September 6
November 17

January 28

**Every day from
6:20 AM to 6:40 AM**

Prayer to Pahaliah

Pahaliah, help me overcome my doubts, fears and obstacles so that I can affirm my vocation.

*Give me the clarity I need
for transforming every defeat into victory
and for drawing out a positive lesson
for the future every time I stumble.*

*Make each of the things that challenge me
a chance for me to surpass myself and make
a profession of faith out of each act that is
inspired by the love of others.*

You were born between July 2 and 6
Your Guardian Angel is

21- Nelchael

HIS ARCHANGEL
Binael

HIS IDENTITY

Gender Male

Family Thrones

HIS AFFINITIES

Stone Carnelian

Candle Red

Incense Musk

Powder Peony

N ELCHAEL symbolizes **victory** over the ups and downs of daily life and **freedom** from existential anxiety. He protects researchers working alone and enhances military strategy when this art is rooted in the notion of duty.

You will call upon him, even if he is not your guardian angel for:

- Finding capital.
- Establishing your ideas.
- Not letting your anxieties stop you.

When to call upon Nelchael?

◆ If Nelchael is your Guardian Angel, you can call upon him and pray to him every day for him to dispense his good deeds on you.

◆ If Nelchael is not your Guardian angel, you can call upon him on his days of regency and 20 minutes every day (see below).

April 10	January 29
June 24	
September 7	Every day from
November 18	6:40 AM to 7:00 AM

Prayer to Nelchael

Nelchael, help me bear the weight of the solitude and duties that weigh down on me.

Reinforce my sense of duty so that I never give up in the face of adversity.

Support each of my efforts so that my attempts are not in vain.

Free me from conventional ideas, and give positive meaning to my mission on this earth.

You were born between July 7 and 11
Your Guardian Angel is

22- Yeiayel

HIS ARCHANGEL
Binael

HIS IDENTITY

Gender Male

Family Thrones

HIS AFFINITIES

Stone Onyx

Candle Brown

Incense Patchouli

Powder Basil

Y EIAYEL symbolizes **goodness and fame**. He encourages his protégés to run away from conflicts and offers them help and assistance against all the collapses that can occur. He contributes to maintaining financial gains, social rank and a good reputation.

You will call upon him, even if he is not your guardian angel for:

◆ Holding onto your place.
◆ Enhancing your finances.
◆ Denouncing gossip.

When to call upon Yeiayel?

◆ If Yeiayel is your Guardian Angel, you can call upon him and pray to him every day for him to dispense his good deeds on you.

◆ If Yeiayel is not your Guardian angel, you can call upon him on his days of regency and 20 minutes every day (see below).

April 11	**January 29**
June 25	
September 8	**Every day from**
November 19	**7:00 AM to 7:20 AM**

Prayer to Yeiayel

Yeiayel, preserve my gains and do not let anyone question
my sense of honor and equity.

Angel of goodness, protect me from conflicts, ugly rumors, envy,
pretenders and false friends.

And if, despite everything, I stumble, hold out a helpful hand to me to ensure the protection of my family and my possessions.

23- *Melahel*

HIS ARCHANGEL
Binael

HIS IDENTITY
Gender Male
Family Thrones

HIS AFFINITIES
Stone Crystal
Candle Green
Incense Camphor
Powder Mint

MELAHEL symbolizes **protection against armed violence** (war, terrorism…). He keeps away violent and accidental death. Protector of nature, he watches over the fertility of the harvests and absolutely loves natural medicine.

You can call upon him even if he is not your guardian angel for:

◆ Avoiding attacks.
◆ Cultivating authenticity.
◆ Having a green thumb.

When to call upon Melahel?

◆ If Melahel is your Guardian Angel, you can call upon him and pray to him every day for him to dispense his good deeds on you.

◆ If Melahel is not your Guardian angel, you can call upon him on his days of regency and 20 minutes every day (see below).

April 12
June 26
September 9
November 20

January 30

Every day from
7:20 AM to 7:40 AM

Prayer to Melahel

Melahel, protect me from attacks, assassination attempts, armed conflicts, and all forms of violence.

Give me the wisdom and vigilance to avoid accidents on the highway.

Guide me in my knowledge of the plants and gifts of Mother Earth so I can live in perfect osmosis with Nature.

You were born between July 17 and 22
Your Guardian Angel is

24- Haheuiah

HIS ARCHANGEL
Binael

HIS IDENTITY

Gender Female

Family Thrones

HIS AFFINITIES

Stone Opal

Candle Silver

Incense Jasmine

Powder Rosemary

HAHEUIAH symbolizes **confidential protection**, the kind that is addressed to stateless people and fugitives. Haheuiah also protects evil animals, vectors of illness, by moving them away from the places where people live.

You can call upon him even if he is not your guardian angel for:

◆ Being naturalized.
◆ Obtaining papers.
◆ Chasing away rats, termites…

When to call upon Haheuiah?

◆ If Haheuiah is your Guardian Angel, you can call upon him and pray to him every day for him to dispense his good deeds on you.

◆ If Haheuiah is not your Guardian angel, you can call upon him on his days of regency and 20 minutes every day (see below).

April 13	**January 31**
June 27	
September 10	**Every day from**
November 21	**7:40 AM to 8:00 AM**

Prayer to Haheuiah

Haheuiah, assign to me a little of your powers so that I may help those who gravitate outside the social fabric to be reintegrated and find their true place.

Help me fight against exclusion, racism, intolerance, prejudices and xenophobia so that the word fraternity begins to have meaning.

Chapter 6

THE 6 ANGELS OF LEO

If you were born between
July 23 and August 23,
your guardian angel is
one of the 6 angels of Leo
and belongs to
the Choir of the Dominations.
Quickly discover his nickname,
special powers
and how to pray to him
to obtain his favors.

You were born between July 23 and 27
Your Guardian Angel is

25- Nith-haiah

HIS ARCHANGEL
Hésediel

HIS IDENTITY

Gender Female

Family Dominations

HIS AFFINITIES

Stone Azurite

Candle Sky blue

Incense Lotus

Powder Sarsaparilla

NITH-HAIAH symbolizes **wisdom and initiation**. He is in the service of ethnic minorities and professions out of the mainstream. This is the angel of astrologers, clairvoyants, mediums, exorcists and people who release others from spells.

Even if Nith-Haiah is not your Guardian angel, you can call upon him for:

◆ Chasing your demons away.
◆ Becoming a medium.
◆ Performing white magic.

Prayer to Nith-haiah

Nith-haiah, protect me from evil and take away from me all forms of influence whether human or occult.

Help me to develop my psychological abilities and to guide people who trust my intuitive capability towards the light.

Have the gifts that heaven has granted me be used in respect and wisdom, without either pride or a mercantilist attitude.

You were born between July 28 and August 1
Your Guardian Angel is

26- Haaiah

HIS ARCHANGEL
Hésediel

HIS IDENTITY
Gender Female

Family Dominations

HIS AFFINITIES
Stone Tanzanite

Candle Mauve

Incense Lotus

Powder Orange tree
flower

HAAIAH symbolizes **truth**. This is the guardian angel that bursts out in a trial as the one closest to the "revelation". He guides future awakened beings and magistrates who apply the law or contribute to promoting it with a concern for equity.

You can call upon him, even if he is not your guardian angel for:

◆ Defending a just cause.
◆ Discovering a truth.
◆ Evolving spiritually.

When to call upon Haaiah?

◆ If Haaiah is your Guardian Angel, you can call upon him and pray to him every day for him to dispense his good deeds on you.

◆ If Haaiah is not your Guardian angel, you can call upon him on his days of regency and 20 minutes every day (see below).

April 15	**February 2**
June 29	
September 12	**Every day from**
November 23	**8:20 AM to 8:40 AM**

Prayer to Haaiah

Haaiah, illuminate my spirit so that I can
distinguish just causes
and arbitrate conflicts
with a concern for equity and harmony.

Inspire me with the solutions
that will enable me to contribute
happiness and peace to those who
call for my help and advice.

You were born between August 2 and 6
Your Guardian Angel is

27- Yératel

HIS ARCHANGEL
Hésediel

HIS IDENTITY

Gender Male

Family Dominations

HIS AFFINITIES

Stone   Diamond

Candle Light blue

Incense Sassafras

Powder Cornflower

ÉRATEL symbolizes **mission and protection**. The mission of propagating the light of faith. Protection against those who attack us. Yératel enhances the social sciences, research, medicine, justice and the arts.

You can call upon him, even if he is not your guardian angel for:

◆ Resolving your problems.
◆ Fulfilling your ideal.
◆ Getting an important position.

When to call upon Yératel?

◆ If Yératel is your Guardian Angel, you can call upon him and pray to him every day for him to dispense his good deeds on you.

◆ If Yératel is not your Guardian angel, you can call upon him on his days of regency and 20 minutes every day (see below).

April 16	**February 3**
June 30	
September 13	**Every day from**
November 24	**8:40 AM to 9:00 AM**

Prayer to Yératel

Yératel, grant me joy, peace
and all the higher qualities
that lead to success.

Free me from my personal
problems so that I am
able to fulfill my mission.

Whether I am the ear that listens,
the voice that reassures and propagates faith,
or the hand that cures bodies in suffering.

You were born between August 7 and 12
Your Guardian Angel is

28- Seheiah

HIS ARCHANGEL
Hésediel

HIS IDENTITY

Gender Female

Family Dominations

HIS AFFINITIES

Stone Blue topaz

Candle Indigo

Incense Star anise

Powder Gardenia

S EHEIAH symbolizes **longevity** and makes sure that everything that could cut life short before its time is avoided: accidents, catastrophes… He guides fire-fighters, rescue workers and doctors and even business people to enable them to manage risks as well as possible. You can call upon him, even if he is not your guardian angel for:

◆ Avoiding accidents.
◆ Protecting you from fire and natural catastrophes.

When to call upon Seheiah?

◆ If Seheiah is your Guardian Angel, you can call upon him and pray to him every day for him to dispense his good deeds on you.

◆ If Seheiah is not your Guardian angel, you can call upon him on his days of regency and 20 minutes every day (see below).

April 17	**February 4**
July 1	
September 14	**Every day from**
November 25	**9:00 AM to 9:20 AM**

Prayer to Seheiah

Seheiah, I put myself under your protection,
Angel of mercy, so that I may travel
in peacefulness and not live in
fear of natural catastrophes,
assassination attempts nor accidents.

Grant me the cool head I need to have
to manage crisis situations
so that I can bring help effectively
to all those who are in distress.

You were born between August 13 and 17
Your Guardian Angel is

29- Reiyel

HIS ARCHANGEL
Hésediel

HIS IDENTITY

Gender Male

Family Dominations

HIS AFFINITIES

Stone Celestite

Candle Light blue

Incense Sandalwood

Powder Blue thistle

R EIYEL symbolizes **strength and power.** He inspires those who have a passion for life and who want to make their often innovative ideas known. Reiyel encourages politicians, visionaries, philosophers, explorers, etc.

You can call upon him, even if he is not your guardian angel for:

◆ Circulating your ideas.
◆ Having ways of knowing.
◆ Astonishing crowds.

When to call upon Reiyel?

◆ If Reiyel is your Guardian Angel, you can call upon him and pray to him every day for him to dispense his good deeds on you.

◆ If Reiyel is not your Guardian angel, you can call upon him on his days of regency and 20 minutes every day (see below).

April 18	**February 5**
July 2	
September 15	**Every day from**
November 26	**9:20 AM to 9:40 AM**

Prayer to Reiyel

Reiyel, angel of knowledge,
enable me to humbly become
the vehicle of your high spirits.

Do not let my ego take over
my mission and my ambitions
supplant my calling.

I want to be the faithful messenger,
in your image, of the divine word
and to use my charisma
for the good of all people.

You were born between August 18 and 22
Your Guardian Angel is

30- Omael

HIS ARCHANGEL
Hésediel

HIS IDENTITY

Gender Male

Family Dominations

HIS AFFINITIES

Stone   Sapphire

Candle   Indigo

Incense Sage

Powder   Narcissus

OMAEL symbolizes **patience and fecundity**. He stimulates his protégés to give preference to human values and to become a source of peace for all those around them. Children and animals will be at the center of their activities. You can call upon him, even if he is not your guardian angel for:

◆ Having a lot of children.
◆ Being a good pedagogue.
◆ Living your life to the full.

When to call upon Omael?

◆ If Omael is your Guardian Angel, you can call upon him and pray to him every day for him to dispense his good deeds on you.

◆ If Omael is not your Guardian angel, you can call upon him on his days of regency and 20 minutes every day (see below).

April 19	**February 6**
July 3	
September 16	**Every day from**
November 27	**9:40 AM to 10:00 AM**

Prayer to Omael

*Omael, grant me many
descendants in perfect physical
and moral health.*

*Breathe into me the right words
to inculcate in them the basic values
of love and sharing.*

*Don't let them wander off their path
and spare them violence, selfishness
and alienating dependencies.*

Chapter 7

THE 6 ANGELS OF VIRGO

If you were born between
August 24 and September 24,
your guardian angel is
one of the 6 angels of Virgo
and belongs to
the Choir of Dominations
or the Choir of Powers.
Quickly discover his nickname,
special powers and
how to pray to him
to obtain his favors.

31- Lécabel

HIS ARCHANGEL
Hésediel

HIS IDENTITY

Gender Female

Family Dominations

HIS AFFINITIES

Stone Florine blue

Candle Blue lagoon

Incense Lotus

Powder Hibiscus

L ÉCABEL symbolizes **talent and glory**. Paradoxically, his protégés are rarely artists but rather astronomers, physicists and researchers who will mark their passage on this earth with a trace of fire and will have every chance of making a fortune.

Even if Lécabel is not your guardian angel, you can call upon him for:

◆ Having your research succeed.
◆ Finding sponsors.
◆ Becoming rich and famous.

When to call upon Lécabel?

◆ If Lécabel is your Guardian Angel, you can call upon him and pray to him every day for him to dispense his good deeds on you.

◆ If Lécabel is not your Guardian angel, you can call upon him on his days of regency and 20 minutes every day (see below).

April 20	**February 7**
July 4	
September 17	**Every day from**
November 28	**10:00 AM to 10:20 AM**

Prayer to Lécabel

Lécabel, give me the ability to have
my head in the stars at the same time
that my feet are on the nourishing ground.

Enable me to find subsidies
so that my ideas and research can come
to fruition since such is my calling.

Bring me fortune, not to enjoy it selfishly,
but to fulfill my ideas
if you judge them useful and just for all.

32- *Vasariah*

HIS ARCHANGEL
Hésediel

HIS IDENTITY

Gender Female

Family Dominations

HIS AFFINITIES

Stone Smoky quartz

Candle Gray

Incense Musk

Powder Elderberry

VASARIAH symbolizes **support and listening**. He enables those who pray to him to get help from the Almighty as well as powerful people down below. He grants protection against any possible attackers. You can call upon Vasariah, even if he is not your guardian angel for:

◆ Knocking on the right doors.
◆ Defending just causes.
◆ Getting a patron interested.
◆ Becoming a decision-maker.

When to call upon Vasariah?

◆ If Vasariah is your Guardian Angel, you can call upon him and pray to him every day for him to dispense his good deeds on you.

◆ If Vasariah is not your Guardian angel, you can call upon him on his days of regency and 20 minutes every day (see below).

April 21	**February 9**
July 5	
September 18	**Every day from**
November 29	**10:20 AM to 10:40 AM**

Prayer to Vasariah

Vasariah, my mission is very heavy:
to be both ear and sword,
he who listens and he who decides,
instill poison for doubt in me.

Lighten my burden, beautiful angel,
by breathing just answers into me
by designating the right people to me
by giving me the means to be
up to my task.

33- Yéhuiah

HIS ARCHANGEL
Camaël

HIS IDENTITY

Gender Female
Family Powers

HIS AFFINITIES

Stone Beryl
Candle Red
Incense Peony
Powder Periwinkle

YÉHUIAH symbolizes **supreme protection**. Protection against all hostile maneuvers from bad intentions to black magic. Yéhuiah influences careers that require intuition: trade, diplomacy, creating a company…

You will call upon him, even if he is not your guardian angel for:

◆ Serving you as a shield.
◆ Finding the right arguments.
◆ Winning in a negotiation.

When to call upon Yéhuiah?

◆ If Yéhuiah is your Guardian Angel, you can call upon him and pray to him every day for him to dispense his good deeds on you.

◆ If Yéhuiah is not your Guardian angel, you can call upon him on his days of regency and 20 minutes every day (see below).

April 22 and 23   **February 9**
July 6
September 19   **Every day from**
November 30   **10:40 AM to 11 AM**

Prayer to Yéhuiah

Yéhuiah, give me the intuition and clarity that will enable me to discern the influences, human or occult, that aim to destabilize me every time they are used.

My activities require negotiations that are often hard and, in spite of me, many enemies appear along my road. I therefore ask you for your protection so that I may work, in honor and dignity, without either fears nor compromises.

34- Léhahiah

HIS ARCHANGEL
Camaël

HIS IDENTITY

Gender Female

Family Powers

HIS AFFINITIES

Stone Coral

Candle Orange

Incense Myrrh

Powder Geranium

L ÉHAHIAH symbolizes **self-mastery and good fortune**. He contributes opportunities, social recognition, romantic encounters, etc. to his protégés. Léhahiah encourages those who work in consulting, whether it is judicial, social, psychological or family-oriented.

You will call upon him, even if he is not your guardian angel for:

◆ Favoring your chances in gambling.

◆ Having fortunate encounters.

◆ Climbing the social ladder.

When to call upon Léhahiah?

◆ If Léhahiah is your Guardian Angel, you can call upon him and pray to him every day for him to dispense his good deeds on you.

◆ If Léhahiah is not your Guardian angel, you can call upon him on his days of regency and 20 minutes every day (see below).

April 24	**February 10**
July 7	
September 20	**Every day from**
December 1	**11 AM to 11:20 AM**

Prayer to Léhahiah

Léhahiah, grant me the mastery
that you dispense to your protégés
and without which all good luck
is illusory or temporary.

Remove all negative thoughts from me
and help me tame luck so that
my life and the lives of the people
close to me is a garden of perfumed roses
without thorns.

35- *Chavaquiah*

HIS ARCHANGEL
Camaël

HIS IDENTITY

Gender Female

Family Powers

HIS AFFINITIES

Stone Topaz

Candle Yellow

Incense Amber

Powder Cumin

CHAVAQUIAH symbolizes **forgiveness and reconciliation**. He gives consensus in often painful questions of inheritance. This angel inspires notaries, educators, children's judges and all those who work to strengthen family ties.

You will call upon him, even if he is not your guardian angel for:

- Inheriting a possession.
- Reconnecting with a relative.
- Finding a child.

When to call upon Chavaquiah?

◆ If Chavaquiah is your Guardian Angel, you can call upon him and pray to him every day for him to dispense his good deeds on you.

◆ If Chavaquiah is not your Guardian angel, you can call upon him on his days of regency and 20 minutes every day (see below).

April 25	**February 11**
July 8 and 9	
September 21	**Every day from**
December 2	**11:20 AM to 11:40 AM**

Prayer to Chavaquiah

Chavaquiah, help me create
a climate of peace around me so that
I may transmit the material and
moral patrimony of which I am the guardian,
with respect for tradition and faith.

May these possessions, fruits of the labor
of our elders, no longer be a factor of discord
but allow those who benefit from them
to develop their inner richness
and always preserve family harmony.

You were born between September 18 and 23
Your Guardian Angel is

36- Menadel

HIS ARCHANGEL

Camaël

HIS IDENTITY

Gender Male

Family Powers

HIS AFFINITIES

Stone Citrine

Candle Yellow

Incense Vanilla

Powder Jonquil

MENADEL symbolizes **accomplishment**. He gives all its meaning to the value of work and ennobles it. Menadel helps all those who want to succeed in their profession, and to make their ideas concrete.

You can call upon him, even if he is not your guardian angel for:

◆ Finding a good job.
◆ Getting a promotion.
◆ Succeeding in your area.
◆ Creating your company.

When to call upon Menadel?

◆ If Menadel is your Guardian Angel, you can call upon him and pray to him every day for him to dispense his good deeds on you.

◆ If Menadel is not your Guardian angel, you can call upon him on his days of regency and 20 minutes every day (see below).

April 26
July 10
September 22
December 3

February 12

Every day from
11:40 AM to 12 PM

Prayer to Menadel

Menadel, help me in my search
for a job where I can be fulfilled
and that I can put myself into totally.

I don't want the major part
of my life to be alienated by a job
that would only be for earning a living.

So help me fulfill myself and find
my rightful place, without worrying about
the efforts or sacrifices it may require of me.

Chapter 8

THE 6 ANGELS OF LIBRA

If you were born between
September 24 and October 22,
your guardian angel is
one of the 6 angels of Libra
and belongs to the Choir of Powers
or the Choir of Qualities.
Quickly find out his nickname,
special powers, and how to pray to him
to obtain their favors.

37- *Aniel*

HIS ARCHANGEL
Camaël

HIS IDENTITY

Gender Male

Family Powers

HIS AFFINITIES

Stone Jasper

Candle Red

Incense Violet

Powder Ginger

ANIEL symbolizes **courage and endurance**. He gives his protégés a pronounced taste for professions involving risk and working on one's own: stuntman, explorer, magus... as well as those that have to do with nature and its secrets.

Even if Aniel is not your guardian angel, you can call upon him for:

◆ Taking off on an adventure.
◆ Winning a car rally, a rodeo...
◆ Being initiated in magic.
◆ Fulfilling your Great Work.

When to call upon Aniel?

◆ If Aniel is your Guardian Angel, you can call upon him and pray to him every day for him to dispense his good deeds on you.

◆ If Aniel is not your Guardian angel, you can call upon him on his days of regency and 20 minutes every day (see below).

April 27	**February 13**
July 11	
September 23	**Every day from**
December 4	**12 PM to 12:20 PM**

Prayer to Aniel

Aniel, give me the strength to fulfill
all my dreams,
to attempt the great adventure
that will expand my horizons.

If I choose a motionless voyage
may my quest be magical or alchemical,
guide it towards the light and spare me
the temptations of Darkness.

You were born between September 29 and October 3, Your Guardian Angel is

38- Haamiah

HIS ARCHANGEL
Camaël

HIS IDENTITY

Gender Female

Family Powers

HIS AFFINITIES

Stone Rhodonite

Candle Red

Incense Amber

Powder Rose

HAAMIAH symbolizes the **Great Love Affair**. Master of the energies of Venus, he gives his protégés the imperious desire to experience extraordinary love. Interest in and understanding of wild animals is also within his competence.

You can call upon him, even if he is not your guardian angel for:

◆ Experiencing a wild love affair.
◆ Becoming veterinarian, trainer.
◆ Firing up your creativity.

When to call upon Haamiah?

◆ If Haamiah is your Guardian Angel, you can call upon him and pray to him every day for him to dispense his good deeds on you.

◆ If Haamiah is not your Guardian angel, you can call upon him on his days of regency and 20 minutes every day (see below).

April 28   **February 14**
July 12
September 24   **Every day from**
December 5   **12:20 PM to 12:40 PM**

Prayer to Haamiah

*Haamiah, guide me so I may find
the exceptional being with whom I will
experience a unique, magical and intensely
close love relationship
in the time of my passing on earth.*

*Enable me to establish a dialogue
with animals, to understand their needs
and their suffering and to bring them help,
love and compassion.*

You were born between October 4 and 8
Your Guardian Angel is

39- *Réhael*

HIS ARCHANGEL
Camaël

HIS IDENTITY

Gender Male

Family Powers

HIS AFFINITIES

Stone Beryl

Candle Light yellow

Incense Vanilla

Powder Orchid

RÉHAEL symbolizes **order and a cure** for diseases of the body and soul. The cure being considered the result of restored order. His protégés have a lively spirit and speed in carrying things out. They are excellent seconds in command. You can call upon him, even if he is not your guardian angel for:

◆ Regaining your health.
◆ Reestablishing family harmony.
◆ Being able to carry out orders well.

When to call upon Réhael?

◆ If Réhael is your Guardian Angel, you can call upon him and pray to him every day for him to dispense his good deeds on you.

◆ If Réhael is not your Guardian angel, you can call upon him on his days of regency and 20 minutes every day (see below).

April 29
July 13
September 25
December 6

February 15

Every day from
12:40 PM to 1:00 PM

Prayer to Réhael

Réhael, give me the clarity I need
so that I can make the right decisions
and carry out the tasks
given by my superiors
with awareness and speed.

Take care of my health and
my family's health,
inspire in me a healthy way of living
and have harmony and well-being prevail
within my family life.

You were born between October 9 and 13
Your Guardian Angel is

40- *Yézalel*

HIS ARCHANGEL
Camaël

HIS IDENTITY

Gender Male

Family Powers

HIS AFFINITIES

Stone Pearl

Candle Pearly

Incense Myrrh

Powder Nettle

ÉZALEL symbolizes **inspiration and aid**. He reveals the part of a creative or artistic genius that lies in his protégés. He favors images and imagination: writing, cinema, publishing, recordings... and frees those from everything that can oppress them.

You can call upon him, even if he is not your guardian angel for:

◆ Writing the story of your life.
◆ Becoming the new star.
◆ Having self-confidence.

When to call upon Yézalel?

◆ If Yézalel is your Guardian Angel, you can call upon him and pray to him every day for him to dispense his good deeds on you.

◆ If Yézalel is not your Guardian angel, you can call upon him on his days of regency and 20 minutes every day (see below).

April 30	**February 16**
July 14	
September 26	**Every day from**
December 7	**1:00 PM to 1:20 PM**

Prayer to Yézalel

Yézalel, give me the assurance I need
for cultivating these artistic gifts
that I feel within me, intuitively,
but which are still lying fallow.

Free me from my inner enemies,
doubt and lack of self-confidence,
and place on my path the gardeners
and masters who will make them bloom.

You were born between October 14 and 18
Your Guardian Angel is

41- Hahahel

HIS ARCHANGEL
Raphaël

HIS IDENTITY

Gender   Male

Family   Qualities

HIS AFFINITIES

Stone   Fiery agate

Candle   Gold

Incense Patchouli

Powder   Sunflower

HAHAHEL symbolizes **the calling and faith** of the spiritual, religious and humanitarian mission. He endows his protégés with great intuition, original ideas, high ideals and exceptional magnetism.

You can call upon the angel Hahahel, even if he is not your guardian angel for:

◆ Accomplishing a mission.
◆ Devoting yourself to a cause.
◆ Providing relief with your hands.

When to call upon Hahahel?

◆ If Hahahel is your Guardian Angel, you can call upon him and pray to him every day for him to dispense his good deeds on you.

◆ If Hahahel is not your Guardian angel, you can call upon him on his days of regency and 20 minutes every day (see below).

May 1	**February 17**
July 15	
September 27	**Every day from**
December 8	**1:20 PM to 1:40 PM**

Prayer to Hahahel

Hahahel, angel of mercy,
guide every one of my words
so that I can convince and
convert the impure and the impious.

Guide every one of my acts
to show the way
to those who doubt.

Guide every one of my gestures
to provide relief and to heal
those who suffer.

You were born between October 19 and 23
Your Guardian Angel is

42- Mikaël

HIS ARCHANGEL
Raphaël

HIS IDENTITY

Gender Male

Family Qualities

HIS AFFINITIES

Stone Serpentine

Candle Honey

Incense Amber

Powder Angelica

MIKAËL symbolizes **moral support and faithfulness**. He stimulates his protégés to use their knowledge and power for constructive ends and lightens up with his light those who must bear a physical or moral load that is heavy and unfair. You can call upon him, even if he is not your guardian angel for:

◆ Finding financial help.
◆ Having your rights be recognized.
◆ Shunning compromises.

When to call upon Mikaël?

◆ If Mikaël is your Guardian Angel, you can call upon him and pray to him every day for him to dispense his good deeds on you.

◆ If Mikaël is not your Guardian angel, you can call upon him on his days of regency and 20 minutes every day (see below).

May 2	**February 18**
July 16	
September 28	**Every day from**
December 9	**1:40 PM to 2:00 PM**

Prayer to Mikaël

Mikaël, my burden is too heavy,
I need your help and compassion,
merciful Angel,
to win out over the obstacles
that appear on my road.

Guide me so that I don't use my knowledge,
through vexation or helplessness,
to dominate and submit others
instead of dominating myself
and submitting myself to your law.

Chapter 9

THE 6 ANGELS OF SCORPIO

If you were born between
October 23 and November 22,
your guardian angel is
one of the 6 angels of Scorpio
and belongs to the Choir of Qualities.
Quickly find out his nickname,
special powers,
and how to pray to him
to obtain his favors.

You were born between October 24 and 28
Your Guardian Angel is

43- Veuliah

HIS ARCHANGEL
Raphaël

HIS IDENTITY
Gender Female
Family Qualities

HIS AFFINITIES
Stone Tiger's eye
Candle Gold
Incense Zinnia
Powder Jonquil

V EULIAH symbolizes **prosperity** in business and **accomplishment** of one's projects. He supports those who have to undertake projects without being weak and which also fall within areas as vast as economy, politics or the army.

You can call upon him, even if he is not your guardian angel for:

◆ Attaining a key position.
◆ Feeling invincible.
◆ Forcing destiny, luck.

When to call upon Veuliah?

◆ If Veuliah is your Guardian Angel, you can call upon him and pray to him every day for him to dispense his good deeds on you.

◆ If Veuliah is not your Guardian angel, you can call upon him on his days of regency and 20 minutes every day (see below).

May 3	**February 19**
July 17	
September 29	**Every day from**
December 10	**2:00 PM to 2:20 PM**

Prayer to Veuliah

Veuliah, have my combativeness
be in the service of your justice
and serve just and noble causes
that will enrich my consciousness.

Preserve me from the hatred that is
a major obstacle to my growth
and grant me the grace of a
lucky and prosperous existence.

44- Yelahiah

HIS ARCHANGEL
Raphaël

HIS IDENTITY

Gender Female

Family Qualities

HIS AFFINITIES

Stone Yellow jasper

Candle Gold

Incense Sandalwood

Powder Coriander

Y ELAHIAH is the Joan of Arc of the angels! He ensures your **physical protection and safety** against breaking and entering and attackers. He breathes the spirit of conquest and great physical strength into his flock.

You can call upon Yelahiah, even if he is not your guardian angel for:

◆ Pushing you into action.
◆ Crowning you with laurels.
◆ Making you invulnerable.

When to call upon Yelahiah?

◆ If Yelahiah is your Guardian Angel, you can call upon him and pray to him every day for him to dispense his good deeds on you.

◆ If Yelahiah is not your Guardian angel, you can call upon him on his days of regency and 20 minutes every day (see below).

May 4	**February 20**
July 18	
September 30	**Every day from**
December 11	**2:20 PM to 2:40 PM**

Prayer to Yelahiah

Yelahiah, give me strength and courage to face my Destiny even if I must take up arms, wear out my strength and weigh down my karma to do that.

My spirit of adventure and conquest often leads me to infringe on divine law without which everything is chaos.

That is why I am counting on you, my guide, to rein in my impetuosity and put me back on the straight path.

45- Sehaliah

HIS ARCHANGEL
Raphaël

HIS IDENTITY
Gender Female
Family Qualities

HIS AFFINITIES
Stone Pyrite
Candle Pale yellow
Incense Lemon balm
Powder Verbena

SEHALIAH symbolizes **success and vitality**. He inspires in his protégés nobility of soul and feelings, keeps them from the effects of lying and meanness and helps them lift themselves above their condition when it is a modest one.

You can call upon him, even if he is not your guardian angel for:

◆ Lifting yourself up socially.
◆ Feeling invulnerable.
◆ Inspiring great feelings in you.

When to call upon Sehaliah?

◆ If Sehaliah is your Guardian Angel, you can call upon him and pray to him every day for him to dispense his good deeds on you.

◆ If Sehaliah is not your Guardian angel, you can call upon him on his days of regency and 20 minutes every day (see below).

May 5   **February 21**

July 19

October 1   **Every day from**

December 12   **2:40 PM to 3:00 PM**

Prayer to Sehaliah

Sehaliah, keep me away from all excesses
so that my vitality is at its zenith.

Give me the means of lifting myself up in
society and satisfying my ambitions.

Grant me the intelligence of the heart that
makes it possible to be heard both
by the humble and the affluent.

Move away from my path of light
evil, envious and miserly people.

You were born between November 8 and 12
Your Guardian Angel is

46- Ariel

HIS ARCHANGEL
Raphaël

HIS IDENTITY
Gender Male
Family Qualities

HIS AFFINITIES
Stone Shiny quartz
Candle Gold
Incense Benzoin
Powder Heliotrope

A RIEL symbolizes **achieving one's ideals**. He helps his protégés make their dreams come true. Ariel breathes new ideas, and makes it possible to shine in society and to deploy boundless seduction. You can call upon Ariel, even if he is not your guardian angel for:

◆ Discovering a treasure in oneself.
◆ Having a devastating charm.
◆ Shining through your intelligence.
◆ Achieving all your goals.

When to call upon Ariel?

◆ If Ariel is your Guardian Angel, you can call upon him and pray to him every day for him to dispense his good deeds on you.

◆ If Ariel is not your Guardian angel, you can call upon him on his days of regency and 20 minutes every day (see below).

May 6	**February 22**
July 20	
October 2	**Every day from**
December 13	**3:00 PM to 3:20 PM**

Prayer to Ariel

Ariel, protect me from the disillusions
that lie in wait for those who always
want to go higher.

Help me avoid giving into discouragement
and giving up my ideal
out of fear of future disenchantment.

Help me find the middle ground
and both keep my feet on the ground
and my head in the stars.

47- Asaliah

HIS ARCHANGEL
Raphaël

HIS IDENTITY

Gender Female

Family Qualities

HIS AFFINITIES

Stone Pearl

Candle Gray

Incense Olibanum

Powder Green tea

ASALIAH symbolizes **truth and contemplation**. The truth that one discovers in oneself, and that which one reveals to others. Asaliah offers his protégés brilliant abilities of deduction which sometimes takes them to lead the investigation.

You can call upon him, even if he is not your guardian angel for:

◆ Passing a test.
◆ Finding a sponsor.
◆ Discovering a secret.

When to call upon Asaliah?

◆ If Asaliah is your Guardian Angel, you can call upon him and pray to him every day for him to dispense his good deeds on you.

◆ If Asaliah is not your Guardian angel, you can call upon him on his days of regency and 20 minutes every day (see below).

May 7	**February 23**
July 21	
October 3	**Every day from**
December 14	**3:20 PM to 3:40 PM**

Prayer to Asaliah

Asaliah, open my eyes to help me
discover the events of the past
which, for ages,
have been hidden by people close to me.

Only the truth will make me a free being
able to resolve, in honor
and dignity, the conflictual situations
that line my road.

You were born between November 18 and 22
Your Guardian Angel is

48- Mihael

HIS ARCHANGEL
Raphaël

HIS IDENTITY
Gender Male

Family Qualities

HIS AFFINITIES
Stone Topaz

Candle Gold

Incense Myrrh

Powder Tulip

MIHAEL symbolizes **intuition and love**. He grants his protégés peace, love, friendship and fidelity in relationships. This is the angel who enhances the union of beings and who ensures having descendents and procreating. You can call upon him, even if he is not your guardian angel for:

◆ Being happy in love.
◆ Protecting your family.
◆ Having sincere friends.

When to call upon Mihael?

◆ If Mihael is your Guardian Angel, you can call upon him and pray to him every day for him to dispense his good deeds on you.

◆ If Mihael is not your Guardian angel, you can call upon him on his days of regency and 20 minutes every day (see below).

May 8	**February 24**
July 22	
October 4	**Every day from**
December 15	**3:40 PM to 4:00 PM**

Prayer to Mihael

*Mihael, help me assume my
responsibilities for my tribe.
Grant me wisdom and intuition
for anticipating conflictual situations.*

*Give my life value as an example
to transmit the values of justice and peace,
of love and sharing
to my descendents.*

Chapter 10

THE 6 ANGELS OF SAGITTARIUS

If you were born between
November 23 and December 21,
your guardian angel is
one of the 6 angels of Sagittarius
and belongs to
the Choir of the Principalities.
Quickly discover his nickname,
special powers,
and how to pray to him
to obtain his favors.

49- *Véhuel*

HIS ARCHANGEL
Haniel

HIS IDENTITY

Gender Male

Family Principalities

HIS AFFINITIES

Stone Emerald

Candle Rose

Incense Lotus

Powder Wild rose

V ÉHUEL symbolizes **fame and generosity**. He develops intuition, the aesthetic sense and intelligence of the heart in his protégés. Their gift for literature and art will bring fame and perhaps even glory.

Even if Véhuel is not your guardian angel, you can call upon him for:

◆ Having people like you.
◆ Giving you inspiration.
◆ Crowning your gifts.

When to call upon Véhuel?

◆ If Véhuel is your Guardian Angel, you can call upon him and pray to him every day for him to dispense his good deeds on you.

◆ If Véhuel is not your Guardian angel, you can call upon him on his days of regency and 20 minutes every day (see below).

May 9	**February 25**
July 23	
October 5	**Every day from**
December 16	**4:00 PM to 4:20 PM**

Prayer to Véhuel

Véhuel, you who speak to me in my dreams,
show me the road that will enable me
to enhance my artistic gifts
and to give meaning to my life.

Help me also to protect and cherish
the beings who trust me for even
if succeeding in life would fulfill me,
succeeding in my life in lovingness
is my main ambition.

You were born between November 28 and December 2, Your Guardian Angel is

50- Daniel

HIS ARCHANGEL
Haniel

HIS IDENTITY

Gende Male

Family Principalities

HIS AFFINITIES

Stone Fluorite

Candle Pale green

Incense Djaoui

Powder Magnolia

DANIEL symbolizes **Providence**, the unexpected help of the Almighty, offered without either obligation nor expecting anything in return. Daniel supports those who have to convince people in their profession through their eloquence: lawyers, preachers, philosophers, teachers, etc.

You can call upon him, even if he is not your guardian angel for:

◆ Pulling you through.
◆ Overcoming and convincing.
◆ Getting luck on your side.

When to call upon Daniel?

◆ If Daniel is your Guardian Angel, you can call upon him and pray to him every day for him to dispense his good deeds on you.

◆ If Daniel is not your Guardian angel, you can call upon him on his days of regency and 20 minutes every day (see below).

May 10　　　　　**February 26**
July 24
October 6　　　　**Every day from**
December 17　　　 **4:20 PM to 4:40 PM**

Prayer to Daniel

*Daniel: intercede in my favor
with the Almighty for I am
currently at a dead end.*

*Guide me on the road to success
and give me the charisma needed
to succeed in my professional life.*

*Luck has not been favorable to me
in this last period and I really need
your help for it to smile on me again.*

51- Hahasiah

HIS ARCHANGEL
Haniel

HIS IDENTITY

Gender Male

Family Principalities

HIS AFFINITIES

Stone Tourmaline

Candle Rose

Incense Vanilla

Powder Orchid

HAHASIAH symbolizes **vocation and wisdom**. The elevation of the soul towards mysticism whose mission is to obtain redemption. The vocation in particular is for medicine. He also contributes to major scientific discoveries.

You can call upon Hahasiah, even if he is not your guardian angel for:

◆ Making a vocation concrete.
◆ Getting closer to nature.
◆ Overcoming your dependencies.

When to call upon Hahasiah?

◆ If Hahasiah is your Guardian Angel, you can call upon him and pray to him every day for him to dispense his good deeds on you.

◆ If Hahasiah is not your Guardian angel, you can call upon him on his days of regency and 20 minutes every day (see below).

May 11	**February 27**
July 25	
October 7	**Every day from**
December 18	**4:40 PM to 5:00 PM**

Prayer to Hahasiah

*Hahasiah: help me fulfill
my deepest aspirations.*

*Enhance my research
so that it is useful to all.*

*Give me the strength to pursue my Quest
without falling into discouragement
and alienating dependencies.*

You were born between December 8 and 12
Your Guardian Angel is

52- *Imamiah*

HIS ARCHANGEL
Haniel

HIS IDENTITY

Gender Female

Family Principalities

HIS AFFINITIES

Stone   Citrine

Candle   Honey

Incense   Benzoin

Powder   Mimosa

I MAMIAH symbolizes **protection and respect**. He gives his protégés the chance to turn situations around in their favor. He protects travels. Prisoners and "traveling people" (Gypsies) are placed under his aegis.

You can call upon him, even if he is not your guardian angel for:

◆ Traveling with no danger.
◆ Being freed.
◆ Fighting against exclusion.

When to call upon Imamiah?

◆ If Imamiah is your Guardian Angel, you can call upon him and pray to him every day for him to dispense his good deeds on you.

◆ If Imamiah is not your Guardian angel, you can call upon him on his days of regency and 20 minutes every day (see below).

May 12	**February 28**
July 26	
October 8	**Every day from**
December 19	**5:00 PM to 5:20 PM**

Prayer to Imamiah

Imamiah: angel of ethnic minorities,
people who are excluded and outsiders,
open the path of solidarity and tolerance for me.

Enable me to help you for if I am in pain
and need tomorrow,
I know that you will grant me
your protection and your listening.

Protect me when I leave on a trip
and free me forever from the poison
of indifference and selfishness.

You were born between December 13 and 16
Your Guardian Angel is

53- *Nanael*

HIS ARCHANGEL
Haniel

HIS IDENTITY

Gender Male

Family Principalities

HIS AFFINITIES

Stone Fluorite

Candle Yellow

Incense Ylang-ylang

Powder Lemon balm

NANAEL symbolizes **knowledge and inspiration**. The knowledge of esotericism, and methods for lifting the spirit up to higher planes of awareness: dreaming while awake, meditation, or prayer. The inspiration for studying sciences and law.

You can call upon him, even if he is not your guardian angel for:

◆ Drawing luck to you.
◆ Developing your psychological insight.
◆ Seeking truth.

When to call upon Nanael?

◆ If Nanael is your Guardian Angel, you can call upon him and pray to him every day for him to dispense his good deeds on you.

◆ If Nanael is not your Guardian angel, you can call upon him on his days of regency and 20 minutes every day (see below).

May 1	February 29 and
July 27	March 1
October 9	Every day from
December 20	5:20 PM to 5:40 PM

Prayer to Nanael

Nanael: awaken in me that divine spark that enables every person to carry out his task on earth in honor and virtue.

Inspire me with noble feelings and have love and the heart's impulses always be my priorities.

And even if I am distraught don't ever let pettiness or envy darken my path towards the light.

54- Nithael

HIS ARCHANGEL
Haniel

HIS IDENTITY

Gender Male

Family Principalities

HIS AFFINITIES

Stone Pearl

Candle Silver

Incense Iris

Powder Lily

N ITHAEL symbolizes **beauty and art**. He grants his protégés a happy life and shelters them from thieves and swindlers. He influences careers that fall within the wake of stars and crowned heads.

You can call upon him, even if he is not your guardian angel for:

◆ Succeeding in artistic photography.
◆ Rubbing shoulders with celebrities.
◆ Getting into the jet set.
◆ Entering into the light.

When to call upon Nithael?

◆ If Nithael is your Guardian Angel, you can call upon him and pray to him every day for him to dispense his good deeds on you.

◆ If Nithael is not your Guardian angel, you can call upon him on his days of regency and 20 minutes every day (see below).

May 14	**March 2**
July 28	
October 10	**Every day from**
December 21	**5:40 PM to 6:00 PM**

Prayer to Nithael

Nithael: spare me the pitfalls
that dominate in this world of glitter
and gloss where I am evolving
with the fascination
of a butterfly in the light.

I love to create beauty and illusion, of course,
but I can not submit to their fascination.
That is why I ask you to help me
not forget basic values.

Chapter 11

THE 6 ANGELS OF CAPRICORN

If you were born between
December 22 and January 20,
your guardian angel is
one of the 6 angels of Capricorn
and belongs to
the Choir of Principalities
and the Choir of Angels – Archangels.
Quickly discover his nickname,
his special powers
and how to pray to him
to obtain his favors.

You were born between December 22 and 26
Your Guardian Angel is

55- *Mébahiah*

HIS ARCHANGEL
Haniel

HIS IDENTITY

Gender Female

Family Principalities

HIS AFFINITIES

Stone   Peridot

Candle   Ivory

Incense   Apple

Powder   Angelica

M ÉBAHIAH symbolizes **morals**. He participates in spreading spiritual ideas and gives our consumer society access to other levels of consciousness. He also protects children, facilitating procreation and watching over their education. Even if he is not your guardian angel, you can call upon Mébahiah for:

◆ Enlarging your family.
◆ Having a dialogue with the angels.
◆ Putting yourself into a task.

When to call upon Méhabiah?

◆ If Méhabiah is your Guardian Angel, you can call upon him and pray to him every day for him to dispense his good deeds on you.

◆ If Méhabiah is not your Guardian angel, you can call upon him on his days of regency and 20 minutes every day (see below).

May 15	**March 3**
July 29	
October 11	**Every day from**
December 22	**6:00 PM to 6:20 PM**

Prayer to Mébahiah

Mébahiah, give me the moral and spiritual strength to accomplish my mission.

Don't let me sink into substance and earthly pleasures.

Have me be an example for my children and people close to me.

Facilitate my contacts with the other levels so that I may become the witness and the flame.

56- Poyel

HIS ARCHANGEL
Haniel

HIS IDENTITY

Gender Male

Family Principalities

HIS AFFINITIES

Stone Tourmaline

Candle Rose

Incense Patchouli

Powder Crocus

POYEL symbolizes **knowledge and power**. He grants his protégés the gift of eloquence that leads them to fame. He protects writers, screenwriters, linguists, singers and opera composers.

You can call upon him, even if he is not your guardian angel for:

◆ Becoming famous.
◆ Making a living from your Art.
◆ Being verbally gifted.

When to call upon Poyel?

◆ If Poyel is your Guardian Angel, you can call upon him and pray to him every day for him to dispense his good deeds on you.

◆ If Poyel is not your Guardian angel, you can call upon him on his days of regency and 20 minutes every day (see below).

May 16	**March 4**
July 30 and 31	
October 12	**Every day from**
December 23	**6:20 PM to 6:40 PM**

Prayer to Poyel

Poyel: you give concrete expression to lunar
and Venusian energies,
grant me a parcel
of your beneficent light so that
I may become the word that enchants people
and brings joy to people's hearts.

Let the music of words and notes
reunite with the music of the spheres
to awaken people's consciousness and bring
your message of love and harmony to all.

You were born between January 1 and 5
Your Guardian Angel is

57- Nemamiah

HIS ARCHANGEL
Mikaël

HIS IDENTITY

Gender Female

Family Archangels

HIS AFFINITIES

Stone Jade

Candle Gray

Incense Musk

Powder Almond tree

NEMAMIAH symbolizes **the prosperity** of possessions acquired through work and **the qualities of being in command.** He inspires innovative ideas and enhances scientific, air and spatial and related technologies. You can call upon him, even if he is not your guardian angel for:

◆ Launching an ambitious project.
◆ Earning your spurs as a leader.
◆ Having great ideas.
◆ Communicating easily.

When to call upon Nemamiah?

◆ If Nemamiah is your Guardian Angel, you can call upon him and pray to him every day for him to dispense his good deeds on you.

◆ If Nemamiah is not your Guardian angel, you can call upon him on his days of regency and 20 minutes every day (see below).

May 17
August 1
October 13
December 24

March 5

Every day from
6:40 PM to 7:00 PM

Prayer to Nemamiah

Nemamiah, give me courage
to confront my responsibilities.

Give me the authority that inspires respect
without engendering fear.

Enable me to calmly enjoy
the fruits of my labor.

Inspire me with innovative ideas for
facilitating communication between people.

You were born between January 6 and 10
Your Guardian Angel is

58- Yeyalel

HIS ARCHANGEL
Mikaël

HIS IDENTITY

Gender Female

Family Archangels

HIS AFFINITIES

Stone Obsidian

Candle Gray

Incense Amber

Powder Bergamot

orange

Y EYALEL symbolizes **cures** for all illnesses, but especially from psychological disturbances. He also symbolizes fighting waged to root out evil or manipulative beings.

You can call upon him, even if he is not your guardian angel for:

◆ Getting a cure.
◆ Punishing an attacker.
◆ Confounding a sorcerer.

When to call upon Yeyalel?

◆ If Yeyalel is your Guardian Angel, you can call upon him and pray to him every day for him to dispense his good deeds on you.

◆ If Yeyalel is not your Guardian angel, you can call upon him on his days of regency and 20 minutes every day (see below).

May 18
August 2
October 14
December 25

March 6

Every day from
7:00 PM to 7:20 PM

Prayer to Yeyalel

Yeyalel, protect me as well as those who are dear to me from illnesses that affect the body or the mind.

Give me the strength of character to reject all forms of influence whether human or occult.

And if despite everything, I am struck, enable me to confound those who infringe on divine laws by practicing black magic.

You were born between January 11 and 15
Your Guardian Angel is

59- Harael

HIS ARCHANGEL
Mikaël

HIS IDENTITY

Gender Male

Family Archangels

HIS AFFINITIES

Stone Magnetite

Candle Slate gray

Incense Lavender

Powder Chamomile

HARAEL symbolizes **wisdom and submission** to administrative hierarchy, the spirit of the laws and writings. He enhances publishing, printing and archives that will be the memory of future generations. You can call upon Harael, even if he is not your guardian angel for:

◆ Having access to culture.
◆ Transmitting your knowledge.
◆ Being in politics.

When to call upon Harael?

◆ If Harael is your Guardian Angel, you can call upon him and pray to him every day for him to dispense his good deeds on you.

◆ If Harael is not your Guardian angel, you can call upon him on his days of regency and 20 minutes every day (see below).

May 19	**March 7**
August 3	
October 15	**Every day from**
December 26	**7:20 PM to 8:00 PM**

Prayer to Harael

*Harael, enable me not to give in
to facility in just becoming a pen pusher,
a simple book – related worker or
researcher working for an administration.*

*Give more nobility to my ambitions
and enable me to become the memory
of my time while I collect written material
to transmit it to future generations.*

Give me a destiny!

You were born between January 16 and 20
Your Guardian Angel is

60- Mitzrael

HIS ARCHANGEL
Mikaël

HIS IDENTITY

Gender Male

Family Archangels

HIS AFFINITIES

Stone Opal

Candle Silver

Incense Oliban

Powder Verbena

MITZRAEL symbolizes **being cured from mental illnesses** and personality disorders. He enhances all careers that work towards preventing them and healing them. He is the angel of psychologists, neurologists, nurses, etc.

You can call upon him, even if he is not your guardian angel for:

◆ Helping someone depressed be cured.
◆ Following the traces of Dr Jekyll.
◆ Not becoming M. Hyde!

When to call upon Mitzrael?

◆ If Mitzrael is your Guardian Angel, you can call upon him and pray to him every day for him to dispense his good deeds on you.

◆ If Mitzrael is not your Guardian angel, you can call upon him on his days of regency and 20 minutes every day (see below).

May 20	**March 8**
August 4	
October 16	**Every day from**
December 27	**7:40 PM to 8:00 PM**

Prayer to Mitzrael

Mitzrael, grant me staunch mental health
so that I can help
those whose mind wanders.

Protect those who are dear to me from
drifting emotionally, having gloomy ideas
and chronic depressive states.

Develop in me the sense of listening
and inspire me with the right words
that relieve and heal people.

Chapter 12

THE 6 ANGELS OF AQUARIUS

If you were born between
January 21 and February 18,
your guardian angel is
one of the 6 angels of Aquarius.
He belongs to the Angels-Archangels
or the Choir of Angels-Angels.
Quickly discover his nickname,
his special powers,
and how to pray to him
to obtain his favors.

61- Umabel

HIS ARCHANGEL
Mikaël

HIS IDENTITY

Gender Male

Family Archangels

HIS AFFINITIES

Stone Amethyst

Candle Blue gray

Incense Vetiver

Powder Lavender

U MABEL symbolizes **memory and detachment**. He enhances fast training and knowledge of the sciences, in particular of physics and astronomy. Umabel grants comfort for love's pain and sorrow.

Even if he is not your guardian angel, you can call upon him for:

◆ Having access to knowledge.
◆ Avoiding a breakup.
◆ Soothing heartache.

When to call upon Umabel?

◆ If Umabel is your Guardian Angel, you can call upon him and pray to him every day for him to dispense his good deeds on you.

◆ If Umabel is not your Guardian angel, you can call upon him on his days of regency and 20 minutes every day (see below).

May 21	**March 9**
August 5	
October 17	**Every day from**
December 28	**8:00 PM to 8:20 PM**

Prayer to Umabel

*Umabel, angel of friendship and
deep feelings, sooth my pain
when my heart is aching.*

*Guide my steps towards the light of knowledge
so that my work is useful to all
and shines like a beacon in the night.*

*May your wisdom illuminate my soul
so that my future becomes the crucible
for a true, serene love relationship.*

62- Iahhel

HIS ARCHANGEL
Mikaël

HIS IDENTITY

Gender Female

Family Archangels

HIS AFFINITIES

Stone Carnelian

Candle Blackish-brown

Incense Amber

Powder Dill

IAHHEL symbolizes **happiness and wisdom**. His protégés bring together qualities of the heart and mind. They don't judge and don't criticize, for they understand human weaknesses.

Even if Iahhel is not your guardian angel, you can call upon him for:

◆ Giving rise to confidences.
◆ Bringing comfort.
◆ Inspiring a great love relationship.
◆ Earning everyone's esteem.

When to call upon Iahhel?

◆ If Iahhel is your Guardian Angel, you can call upon him and pray to him every day for him to dispense his good deeds on you.

◆ If Iahhel is not your Guardian angel, you can call upon him on his days of regency and 20 minutes every day (see below).

May 22	**March 10**
August 6	
October 18	**Every day from**
December 29	**8:20 PM to 8:40 PM**

Prayer to Iahhel

Iahhel, breathe into me that
spirit of tolerance which enables someone
to receive the most painful
or shocking confidences
without criticizing through a hasty verdict.

Open my heart to compassion
and make my advice be useful
to those who ask for it and let it help them,
without overwhelming them,
to find the right path.

You were born between January 31 and February 4, Your Guardian Angel is

63- *Anauel*

HIS ARCHANGEL
Mikaël

HIS IDENTITY

Gender Female

Family Archangels

HIS AFFINITIES

Stone   Pearl

Candle Pearl gray

Incense Bergamot orange

Powder Hawthorn

ANAUEL symbolizes **courage and health**. He grants protection against deadly accidents and cures illnesses. He directs his protégés towards management positions and encourages trade, banking, the economic and advertising sectors.

Even if he is not your guardian angel, you can call upon him for:

◆ Traveling without fear.
◆ Betting on the right horse.
◆ Having ideas and being in top shape.

When to call upon Anauel?

◆ If Anauel is your Guardian Angel, you can call upon him and pray to him every day for him to dispense his good deeds on you.

◆ If Anauel is not your Guardian angel, you can call upon him on his days of regency and 20 minutes every day (see below).

May 23	**March 11**
August 7	
October 19	**Every day from**
December 30	**8:40 PM to 9:00 PM**

Prayer to Anauel

Anauel, give me the courage to fight against the blows of fate and illness.

Protect me as well as people close to me from unexpected accidents.

Grant me discernment for investing in good ideas and good people.

Facilitate my professional success and open the doors of success for me.

You were born between February 5 and 9
Your Guardian Angel is

64- Méhiel

HIS ARCHANGEL
Mikaël

HIS IDENTITY

Gender Male

Family Archangels

HIS AFFINITIES

Stone Jade

Candle Ivory

Incense Lourdes

Powder Sage

MÉHIEL symbolizes **inspiration and prosperity**. He supports careers that have to do with writing and grants fame to writers. Teaching, medicine, trade and leisure activities are also under his protection.

Even if Méhiel is not your guardian angel, you can call upon him for:

◆ Being inspired by the muses.
◆ Becoming rich and famous.
◆ Being a born businessman.

When to call upon Méhiel?

◆ If Méhiel is your Guardian Angel, you can call upon him and pray to him every day for him to dispense his good deeds on you.

◆ If Méhiel is not your Guardian angel, you can call upon him on his days of regency and 20 minutes every day (see below).

May 24 and 25   **March 12**
August 8
October 20   **Every day from**
December 31   **9:00 PM to 9:20 PM**

Prayer to Méhiel

Méhiel, bring me success
in the path that I have chosen.

Help me to fulfill myself fully
in my personal and professional life.

Protect those I love so that their
life is a long calm river.

Enable me to fulfill myself spiritually
so that I can dance in the light.

65- *Damabiah*

HIS ARCHANGEL
Gabriel

HIS IDENTITY

Gender Female

Family Angels

HIS AFFINITIES

Stone Emerald

Candle Green

Incense Amber

Powder St-Johns-wort

DAMABIAH symbolizes **success and protection**. Success in undertakings that are useful and beneficial to others. Protection against sorcery and witchcraft as well as against ordeals.

Even if he is not your guardian angel, you can call upon Damabiah for:

◆ Putting yourself into a mission.
◆ Coming out of ordeals unscathed.
◆ Not having an evil spell be cast against you.
◆ Helping people who are suffering.

When to call upon Damabiah?

◆ If Damabiah is your Guardian Angel, you can call upon him and pray to him every day for him to dispense his good deeds on you.
◆ If Damabiah is not your Guardian angel, you can call upon him on his days of regency and 20 minutes every day (see below).

May 26	**March 13**
August 9	
October 21	**Every day from**
January 1	**9:20 PM to 9:40 PM**

Prayer to Damabiah

Damabiah, engender
the spirit of compassion in me
which is part of your divine essence.

Invest me with a humanitarian
or charitable mission
that gives meaning to my life.

Protect me against all
forms of evil spells and help me
overcome all ordeals.

You were born between February 15 and 19
Your Guardian Angel is

66- *Manakel*

MANAKEL symbolizes **freedom and relief** for one's guilt feelings connected to the past. He inspires those who are interested in the meaning of dreams and the unconscious and those who practice prenatal and postnatal medicine for children. Even if he is not your guardian angel, you can call upon Manakel for:

◆ Becoming a psychologist or pediatrician.
◆ Freeing yourself form the past.
◆ Healing a sick child.

When to call upon Manakel?

◆ If Manakel is your Guardian Angel, you can call upon him and pray to him every day for him to dispense his good deeds on you.

◆ If Manakel is not your Guardian angel, you can call upon him on his days of regency and 20 minutes every day (see below).

May 27	**March 14**
August 10	
October 22	**Every day from**
January 2	**9:40 PM to 10:00 PM**

Prayer to Manakel

Manakel, help me make a clean sweep of the miasmas of the past and turn towards the future confidently.

Reveal the meaning of my destiny to me through dreams and teach me how to decipher them without making mistakes.

Guide my relationships with children so that I can plant the promise of better days in their lives.

Chapter 13

THE 6 ANGELS OF PISCES

If you were born between
February 19 and March 20,
your guardian angel is
one of the 6 angels of Pisces.
He belongs to
the Choir of the Angels-Angels.
Quickly discover his nickname,
his special powers,
and how to pray to him
to obtain his favors.

67- Eyael

HIS ARCHANGEL
Gabriel

HIS IDENTITY

Gender Female

Family Angels

HIS AFFINITIES

Stone Lunar

Candle Green

Incense Sandalwood

Powder Spotted lily

E YAEL symbolizes **Knowledge**. His field of influence is vast for he supports philosophers, physicists, astrologers, antique dealers, archeologists, and those all who are passionate about esotericism.

Even if Eyael is not your guardian angel, you can call upon him for:

- ◆ Having revelations.
- ◆ Becoming a candidate initiate.
- ◆ Bringing up the past.

When to call upon Eyael?

◆ If Eyael is your Guardian Angel, you can call upon him and pray to him every day for him to dispense his good deeds on you.

◆ If Eyael is not your Guardian angel, you can call upon him on his days of regency and 20 minutes every day (see below).

May 28	**March 15**
August 11	
October 23	**Every day from**
January 3	**10:00 PM to 10:20 PM**

Prayer to Eyael

*Eyael, guide me on the path of knowledge
and reveal to me
the secrets that will enable me
to become an awakened being.*

*Help me to choose a good master
who is not a guru
and to share my findings with a group
that is not a cult.*

68- Habuhiah

HIS ARCHANGEL
Gabriel

HIS IDENTITY

Gender Female

Family Angels

HIS AFFINITIES

Stone Hematite

Candle Green

Incense Valerian

Powder Hawthorn

H ABUHIAH symbolizes **a cure** for all illnesses, **fecundity** for women and animal and vegetable **fertility**. He protects all those who contribute to giving life: gynecologists, obstetricians, midwives and all those professions that are in contact with Mother Nature. Even if he is not your guardian angel, you can call upon him for:

◆ Overcoming sterility.
◆ Fertilizing the harvests.
◆ Obtaining a cure.

When to call upon Habuhiah?

◆ If Habuhiah is your Guardian Angel, you can call upon him and pray to him every day for him to dispense his good deeds on you.

◆ If Habuhiah is not your Guardian angel, you can call upon him on his days of regency and 20 minutes every day (see below).

May 29	**March 16**
August 12	
October 24	**Every day from**
January 4	**10:20 PM to 10:40 PM**

Prayer to Habuhiah

*Habuhiah, angel of cures
and love, protect my health
and the health of everyone close to me.*

*Grant me the power
of producing beautiful children
who will honor my line.*

*Fertilize the nourishing earth
so that people don't have food shortages
any longer, nor are hungry.*

You were born between March 1 and 5
Your Guardian Angel is

69- *Rochel*

HIS ARCHANGEL
Gabriel

HIS IDENTITY
Gender Male

Family Angels

HIS AFFINITIES
Stone Agate

Candle Beige

Incense Myrrh

Powder Passionflower

ROCHEL symbolizes **searching and honesty**. He makes it possible to find what we have lost, both in esteem as well as our possessions. He is an angel that brings luck that contributes to the appearance of fortune, inheritances and gifts.

Even if Rochel is not your guardian angel, you can call upon him for:

◆ Winning at games of chance.
◆ Regaining self-confidence.
◆ Benefiting from a gift.

When to call upon Rochel?

◆ If Rochel is your Guardian Angel, you can call upon him and pray to him every day for him to dispense his good deeds on you.

◆ If Rochel is not your Guardian angel, you can call upon him on his days of regency and 20 minutes every day (see below).

May 30	**March 17**
August 13	
October 25	**Every day from**
January 5	**10:40 PM to 11:00 PM**

Prayer to Rochel

Rochel, let me find
what I lost in the past so that I am,
once again, a whole being.

Give me back my original integrity
by having me discover my soul mate,
my other half that I am lacking.

Have my life take a new leap forward
By bringing luck into
games of love and of chance.

70- Jabamiah

HIS ARCHANGEL
Gabriel

HIS IDENTITY
Gender Female
Family Angels

HIS AFFINITIES
Stone Tanzanite
Candle Green
Incense Sandalwood
Powder Gentian

J ABAMIAH symbolizes **regenerating one's body**. He makes it possible to recover our bodily functions when they have been struck by illness. It is logical then that Jabamiah contributes to geriatricians, biologists, plasticians, physical therapists, etc. Even if he is not your guardian angel, you can call upon him for:

◆ Preserving your integrity.
◆ Optimizing physical therapy.
◆ Avoiding devastating surgical interventions.

Prayer to Jabamiah

*Jabamiah, protect me from accidents
and mutilating illnesses.
Give me the talent for bandaging
and repairing bodies in pain
and accidental devastating effects.
But forbid me from playing Dr. Faust,
as a patient or as someone officiating,
for if beauty and youth are ephemeral
a blow from an unfortunate surgeon's knife
is not.*

71- Haiaiel

HIS ARCHANGEL
Gabriel

HIS IDENTITY

Gender Female

Family Angels

HIS AFFINITIES

Stone Jade

Candle Green

Incense Licorice

Powder Lemon

HAIAIEL symbolizes **courage and peace**. He enhances careers in the military or police work as well as those of firefighters, rescue workers, soldiers of the UN's forces, etc. Even if he is not your guardian angel, you can call upon him for:

◆ Following the flights of your heart.

◆ Saving human lives.

◆ Working in the humanitarian domain.

◆ Becoming the mediator for lost causes.

When to call upon Haiaiel?

◆ If Haiaiel is your Guardian Angel, you can call upon him and pray to him every day for him to dispense his good deeds on you.
◆ If Haiaiel is not your Guardian angel, you can call upon him on his days of regency and 20 minutes every day (see below).

June 1	March 19
August 15	
October 27	Every day from
January 7	11:20 PM to 11:40 PM

Prayer to Haiaiel

Hahaiel, give me the courage
to defend the weak and oppressed
even if that forces me to take
illicit roads.

Give me the right words
for defending lost causes
And for having the righteousness
of the humble and poor triumph.

You were born between March 16 and 20
Your Guardian Angel is

72- Mumiah

HIS ARCHANGEL
Gabriel

HIS IDENTITY

Gender Female

Family Angels

HIS AFFINITIES

Stone Amethyst

Candle Green

Incense Amber

Powder Agrimoine

MUMIAH symbolizes **revelation and perseverance**. The revelation of the secrets of nature that grace us with blessings, as well as the revelation of the secrets of medical science, and the sciences of physics and chemistry.

Even if he is not your guardian angel, you can call upon him for:

◆ Becoming a healer.
◆ Doing chemistry.
◆ Living close to nature.

When to call upon Mumiah?

◆ If Mumiah is your Guardian Angel, you can call upon him and pray to him every day for him to dispense his good deeds on you.

◆ If Mumiah is not your Guardian angel, you can call upon him on his days of regency and 20 minutes every day (see below).

June 2   March 20
August 16
October 28   Every day from
January 8   11:40 PM to Midnight

Prayer to Mumiah

Mumiah, grant me the power
to discover the secrets of the Ancients.

Those of the plants that heal.
those of the blessings of the moon
and the sun.

Those of the stones and the metals
filled with precious trace elements.

Make a medicine man out of me,
a being full of knowledge and wisdom.

Conclusion

THE ANGELS, YOUR GOOD GENIES

T he angel flood which, from books to seminars, from TV broadcasts to Internet sites, promises us wonders of all kinds is not very catholic, we must say! As a matter of fact, the 72 Guardian Angels of the Cabala that you have just gotten to know are, in reality, 72 Genies that have been revamped to win you over.

All you have to do to see it, is to get out the originals of the reference books (especially those of the most famous and prolific of the "angelogists", **Haziel**) and to observe the changes in the titles that have happened these past ten years.

Why this subterfuge?

First of all, to ride of the wave of a successful book: *Inquiry on the Existence of Guardian Angels* by **Pierre Jovanovich**. He takes up the theses and testimonials that have come out of the American New Age which relaunched the phenomenon, in a spirit that was very inspired by paganism.

In this book, guardian angels have no name and only have a very distant relationship with the pious images of the first communicants. They belong more to the demons that are familiar to sorcerers: the servants. All you have to do is to call them (*hey there, do you hear me?..*). Their goal is to turn themselves inside out to satisfy our material desires (often ridiculous or cowardly ones!): finding a parking spot, a taxi at rush hour, the right numbers in the lottery...

Second of all, for respectability. Actually, for many people, owing your taxi or your success in the Lottery to the intervention of your guardian angels is more comfortable than owing it to a disciple of the big Creator in the Sky!

In reality, none of that is important for whatever your beliefs and ideas on the subject, the name of your guardian angel is essential. It is a power word, a mantra, and a support for positive (and creative) thinking, which definitely opens for you — no doubt about it — doors to other levels of consciousness.

So, angels, genies, entities... whatever, the basic thing, my friends, is to open up the airlock that leads to the fulfillment of your desires. For that, knowing the name of your angel is definitely an effective key for making *a paradise on earth* out of your life.

TABLE OF CONTENTS

Chapter 6

Chapter 7

Chapter 8

Chapter 9

Chapter 10

Chapter 11

Chapter 12

Chapter 13